MY GOD:

Abbé Pierre
with Frédéric Lenoir

WHY, OH WHY, MY GOD?

Meditations on Christian faith and the meaning of life

Translated by
Carolyn and William A. McComish

Risk
BOOK SERIES

WCC Publications, Geneva

*The views expressed in this book do not necessarily reflect
those of the World Council of Churches.*

Cover design: Marie Arnaud Snakkers

ISBN 978-2-8254-1707-8

Translated from the original French
Mon Dieu... pourquoi?
℗ Plon, 2005

© 2007, WCC Publications,
for this English translation
World Council of Churches
150 route de Ferney, P. O. Box 2100
1211 Geneva 2, Switzerland

Website: http://www.wcc-coe.org

No. 116 in the Risk Book Series

Printed in France by Lussaud
This printer has a green label guaranteeing environmentally-friendly printing procedures.

Table of Contents

vi

From the translators

As a Presbyterian minister active in the work of the Emmaus community foundation in Geneva, I first met Abbé Pierre some 15 years ago. Long-term and perhaps unlikely friend, I gladly accepted his request to translate this little book into English.

When I became dean of the Reformed cathedral in Geneva, the abbé accepted my invitation to preach at the ecumenical worship service for the Week of Prayer for Christian Unity in 1999 and brought tears to the eyes of the members of the congregation assembled in Calvin's own cathedral of Saint-Pierre (Saint Peter). After the emotion of the ecumenical service (in which the then general secretary of the World Council of Churches, Rev. Dr Konrad Raiser, and Orthodox WCC staff member Fr Ion Bria also participated) the enormous congregation streamed out into the square to find that the Emmaus community had set up chairs, sofas and tables, and were serving coffee.

This event did not make me any friends in the more narrow-minded "Protestant" circles around Saint-Pierre, especially since the abbé preached from Calvin's pulpit, but I am proud to share the abbé's rebellious spirit. The abbé subsequently participated in several celebrations at Saint-Pierre, notably on the occasion of the visit of Kofi Annan, general secretary of the United Nations, and at the signing of the Geneva Spiritual Appeal.

I have found strong echoes of Protestant theology in my own discussions with the abbé and in this book. These ideas are disseminated in the kind of language any reader can understand: not the language of the classical, academic theologian but the language of a pastor who has lived among ordinary people, Christian and non-Christian alike. Jesus used simple language and stories in talking to his audience of peasants, tax collectors and fishermen. The abbé follows his example.

We should be indebted to Frédéric Lenoir for his talent and assiduity in interpreting and recording his talks with the abbé and enabling the publication of *Mon Dieu...pourquoi?* He is the director of the French magazine "Le Monde des religions" (The World of Religions).

I hope Carolyn and I have done justice to this remarkable book.

William A. McComish
Geneva, August 2006

Foreword

Abbé Pierre celebrated his 93rd birthday in 2004. As a young Capuchin (Franciscan) novice, barely 17 years old and impatient to meet God, he prayed for the benediction of an early death.

He "heard" a voice from inside himself reply: "You are not leaving!" Only God knows if it was to punish him for his impatience or to allow him to become a great witness to God's compassion. He was recently voted by viewers of French television as one of the three most important figures in French history (after General de Gaulle and Marie Curie). He is a moral reference to the French nation.

If the founder of Emmaus is already part of our collective conscience, it is first and foremost because he is one of "God's rebels" who, while a believer, refuses to accept poverty and suffering and dedicates his life to making this world a little more humane. I am convinced that it is also because he is a free spirit. Through his numerous public statements he disturbs, he irritates, he questions, he upsets the status quo. No dogma or public institution finds favour in his eyes. His intelligence and sense of indignation are always on the alert. This critical spirit which spares neither the pope nor the president of the French Republic nor the great, fashionable thinkers renders him always worth hearing.

I got to know the Abbé Pierre for the first time some 15 years ago while conducting a long interview with him for a book on the resurgence of ethical concerns. For some years he had lived in his monastic retreat of Saint-Wandrille. He was not able to stay there very long because he was overly solicited by his companions of Emmaus and by the media. He now lives in a very small apartment in the suburbs of Paris, close to the headquarters of the Emmaus organization.

From this first meeting, an intellectual complicity developed between us and we have met quite regularly. While from different generations and experience, we like to discuss philosophy and religion with no other goal than seeking the truth and challenging each other's point of view. Since I had written my doctoral thesis on Buddhism, he often questioned me on this particular tradition, in which he is very interested, particularly since he has had many friendly and stimulating exchanges with the Dalai Lama. We have sometimes been in complete disagreement, for example over the Garaudy affair[1], but these differences have not impaired our friendship.

Sometimes, these exchanges have been of a more professional nature. Twice I have helped the abbé to write his books: his autobiography

---

[1] A former French Communist leader, philosopher and convert to Revisionism and Islam, in 1998 Roger Garaudy was charged, tried and convicted for writing a semi-Revisionist book on the Holocaust.

(*Mémoire d'un croyant*, Fayard, 1997) and a short work on *Fraternité* (Fayard, 1999). A couple of years ago, the founder of Emmaus asked me to meet him more regularly to discuss certain theological questions which particularly tormented him. He had just discovered that John Paul II had officially recognized the validity of the theory of evolution and this minor revolution had stimulated his desire to take up again his long-term reflection on original sin, evil and the meaning of life. I realized that despite his bad health, the abbé was in a state of intellectual effervescence. Many fundamental questions obsessed him in his old age. I proposed to note down the fruits of our discussions and over a period of about a year, meeting almost weekly, this small book was born. I have eliminated my own questions and views in order to keep only those of the abbé.

This book is neither a treatise nor a statement but rather a series of brief meditations on Christian faith and the sense of human life. Not only does it touch on fundamental points of Christian doctrine, but also on intimate and burning topical subjects such as sexuality and the marriage of priests, the place of women in the church, parenting by same sex partners and the election of a new pope.

Far from being stilted religious propaganda, I believe these meditations represent the essential spiritual and current theological preoccupations of

xii

the founder of the Emmaus community – concerns that are as much, if not more, composed of questions as firm convictions.

Frédéric Lenoir

Prologue

Why so much suffering?

The sufferings of humanity since its creation have always felt like an open wound to me. I recently learned that around eight billion people have been born into the world. How many have had a painful existence, have had to struggle and suffer – and for what? Why, dear God, why?

Dear God, how long will this tragedy continue? All religions teach us that life has meaning. But how many women and men out of all these millions have been able to perceive this meaning? How many, or how few, have been able to achieve a spiritual awareness, an awareness of hope? On the other hand, how many others have had to live like animals, in fear, in poverty, in pain and sickness, fighting for survival? How many have really had the possibility of meditating on the meaning of life?

I am ninety-three years of age and my Christian faith, the centre of my life for the last eighty years, leads me to pose more and more questions. Why, oh Lord, why? What is the world for? What is life for? What is human life for?

1. What is there to live for?

People often ask me: what is the point of life?

Despite all my questions I have one single conviction which has been the fundamental reality of my life since I encountered the reality of God's presence in adoration as a young Capuchin monk. Abandoning logic but with the total conviction of my heart and my faith, I reply: the purpose of life is to learn how to love.

To love means that I am happy when you, the other person, are happy. And when you are unhappy or suffering, then I also suffer.

It is as simple as that. So what I believe is that life is a brief period given to us freely to learn how to love, with the obligation to work against evil.

The meaning of life is that love responds to love. All of creation would be meaningless if there were not this supreme moment when, all of a sudden, two free beings are able to give themselves to each other and to love each other.

2. Love and happiness

Over the years I have come to realize that it is important to distinguish love from happiness.

Even if the joy which accompanies love is stronger than all others and gives us the greatest feeling of happiness, it is fragile and does not prevent us from experiencing suffering. As the Virgin Mary told Bernadette of Lourdes: "In this life I promise to teach you to love but not necessarily to be happy all the time."

All human beings want to be happy. But to live a truly Christian life does not mean to seek happiness at all cost. It is to seek to love even if it is difficult to do so.

In writing this, I am conscious of an aberration which must be avoided at all costs, but which has created a trap for many Christians: that of moral suffering. Contrary to what we have always been taught, merit has no link with suffering. Merit is to be measured against the love which makes us undertake an action and not according to what it costs us.

To seek moral suffering is an abomination and a caricature of the Christian life if it gives rise to the idea that we should seek suffering, or that we should gain merit by suffering because Jesus experienced suffering. No, instead we should take life as it comes and if it is not possible to avoid suffering, then we are better off accepting it in love than to be angry or to run away from it.

3. Attitudes to suffering
   Buddha and Jesus

I am, alas, in agreement with the fundamental concept of the Buddha that all is suffering.

The human condition is one which involves suffering; we all suffer physically, psychologically and morally. We suffer when we desire certain things which do not belong to us and then, when we have them, are afraid of losing them or we suffer when they are gone. Suffering is part of every life.

Yet as a Christian, I cannot come to the same conclusions as Buddha. As far as I have understood from my own reading and through discussion with my friend the Dalai Lama, the Buddhist idea is to do our utmost to avoid suffering. Since the cause of all suffering is desire, the aim of life is to create an asceticism and a strict system of ethics which will eliminate desire.

For the follower of Jesus, the path is totally different. The Christian does not try to eliminate suffering by avoiding desire but rather tries to react to personal desire through sharing and giving. Light shines through when we enter into communion with other people through personal suffering – theirs or ours.

I have often had this awesome experience through personal contact with the very ill or those who have lost all hope. The personal communion with people in these situations brings forth a light that overcomes suffering. Thus suffering can become a springboard which leads us to sharing. Suffering is evil and it should never be sought or exaggerated. But we can reach the highest levels of human emotion through the experience of suffering.

I recently learned that a much respected psychologist, Boris Cyrulnik, noted the same phenomenon in the psychological development of the individual by showing that certain needs and deep wounds from our childhood can help a person to grow and so can be seen as "wonderful misfortunes". This is what I think is true of life in general: that all suffering overcome is a way through which we can grow in spiritual awareness.

4. To desire

Buddhism has led me to reflect deeply about desire.

To try to eliminate desire is, in a way, to reduce, to limit the quality of human life. Unlike Buddha I do not believe that desire is in itself an obstacle to spiritual progress. What I believe is that we should know how to focus our desires.

To be ruled by one's desires can be detrimental. But to be in control of oneself and to move freely towards that which makes us grow, towards that which is good, beautiful and noble, is part of our spiritual development.

I do not believe that anything can ever fully satisfy us on this earth, because our spirit, created by God, is always searching for God. Whether we know it or not, we are always running after all sorts of pleasures that can never be anything but imperfect since the only true pleasure will come from finally meeting with the Eternal. This is what forms the basis of Christian hope. While we are in this world we can, of course, have moments of total pleasure in communion with God or with other people. But these are still only moments which will give way to others when the awareness of communion is less strong, or to periods of frustration.

5. Sexual desire and chastity

When we talk about desire we all think about sexual desire which is one of the most powerful instincts of our lives. If it is not suitably channelled, it can do us much harm. But if it is well directed, that is to say experienced within a true, sharing relationship, it can be very enriching.

When I was very young I chose to dedicate my life to God and to the service of others, and so I took a vow of chastity. To a certain extent, I have lived the life of a captive. When one knows that it is impossible to obtain something that is desired, then it must be set aside. My life as a monk, and then a life totally absorbed by helping the poor, left me no room for amorous relationships. I could not let desire become too important. I call this a willing servitude.

But this does nothing to calm the force of desire, and I have given in to it occasionally. However, I have never had a long-term relationship since I have never allowed sexual desire to take too strong a hold on me. That would have led me to develop a permanent relationship with a woman and would have been contrary to my choice of life. Therefore I have known sexual desire and rare sexual satisfaction, but this satisfaction was a real source of dissatisfaction for I knew that I was not being true to myself.

I believe that sexual desire can be fully satisfactory only in loving, tender and confident relationships. Such relationships were excluded by my way of life. I could only have made women unhappy and would have been torn between two conflicting lifestyles.

6. Celibacy
   and the marriage of priests

Simplicity can only exist in what is true. Hypocrisy, which is too often present, should be rejected. Anyone can give in to sexual desire, which is a very powerful life-force, but it is something quite different for a priest or a monk to be unable to make a clear choice and to live a double life, which in some cases can lead to women suffering over many years.

At the same time, we should avoid all generalizations and all judgement. I know priests who have lived with the woman they love for many years and who accept this situation. They continue to be good priests. But this challenges the church regarding the marriage of priests and the ordination of married men.

If I had been married or if I had been involved in a long-term loving relationship, I could never have achieved what I have done. My calling required a total availability. But I am also convinced that the church needs married priests as well as celibate priests who can devote themselves totally to prayer and to the service of others.

Jesus chose married apostles – like Peter – and also apostles like John who probably remained celibate. The church kept this double form of vocation for centuries before imposing celibacy for priests, which was already the case for bishops. Nowadays married men are ordained not only in the Orthodox churches but also in the Roman Catholic Church in the Coptic and Maronite communities where priests have the choice of being married or celibate.

Since the Roman Catholic Church has for centuries allowed the consecration of married priests in its oriental communities, I cannot understand why John Paul II recently affirmed that it was out of the question to reconsider priestly celibacy for the rest of the church.

This is unacceptable. Such a change would not only help to resolve the lack of vocations for the priesthood and the lack of priests, but I am also convinced that there would always be the same number of vocations for the life of celibacy.

7. The death of John Paul II…

Even if, like many other people, I was not always in agreement with him, I was deeply touched by the death of the pope. I was not shocked by the fact that his last illness was so publicly displayed or that he refused to abdicate. On the contrary, I believe that John Paul II showed great courage in his suffering. I was very moved by the struggle that he made to give his benediction when he could no longer speak. Despite what some people have claimed we know that he remained totally lucid until the end.

What I will not say, unlike many Catholics and even non-Catholics, is that his death saddened me. This is certainly because I have always believed in a new life in God after death. I have never felt a deep sadness on the death of people close to me, not even the deaths of my parents or of Miss Coutaz who was my faithful assistant for thirty-eight years.

I had a curious image of death as a child: I saw a huge wardrobe filled with folded sheets. Everything was in order. Death forms part of the order of events. Since then I have always felt a deep peace when in the presence of death – apart from when I am aware of deaths that take place in appalling suffering. I am shocked not by death itself but by suffering.

This is what I felt about the death of John Paul II. He was a great pope who carried out an enormous task. I had a profound admiration for his humanity, his faith and his total devotion to the church even if, as I have already said, I could not share all his standpoints, especially that of refusing the use of condoms which was appalling given the reality of the African situation.

8. … and the election of Benedict XVI

After the death of John Paul II, everyone was immediately concerned about his successor, and observers feared only one thing: the election of Cardinal Joseph Ratzinger, the redoubtable prefect of the Congregation for the Doctrine of the Faith, the former Holy Office.

I believe that I was among the first to make the sensible observation that wherever a person is promoted to great responsibility in human society, we may see that the person changes. Sometimes the person becomes more authoritarian, but more often the person relaxes, improves and becomes more accommodating. Once at the top a person becomes more tolerant, magnanimous, generous and open-minded.

This is what I believe will happen to Cardinal Ratzinger, now Benedict XVI. When I observed his face on the evening of his election I noted that he was happy and calm. His first words as pope were of dialogue and openness towards the other Christian families – Protestants, Anglicans, Orthodox – and other religions. We must wait to see the results, but the tone has changed.

I was not in the least surprised by his election despite his age, 78, which was not a positive factor. We should remember that not many cardinals know each other. But Cardinal Ratzinger was well known. The chief concern of the cardinals was for stability – no disturbances and no adventures. By electing Joseph Ratzinger they assured continuity with the pontificate of John Paul II, knowing however that, given his age, he was unlikely to reign for too long. This allows them to get to know each other better and to reflect quietly about the best candidate for the next pontificate. It will be at that time that we shall really see what major direction is to be taken.

I shall not be surprised if, during his pontificate, Benedict XVI takes two measures that can be interpreted as liberal: allowing communion for people who have been divorced and who have remarried, as well as the election of "elders", married men who have raised their families and are the famous "presbyters" of whom St Paul writes. On the other hand he will certainly not change his position on the question of the ordination of women or on the condemnation of homosexuality.

9. Homosexual marriage and parenting

Over the last few years there has been much discussion in civil society about homosexual marriage and about the adoption of children by homosexual couples. These are very important questions and I believe that we need time to think about them before legislating on them.

I can well understand the sincere desire of homosexual couples, who have often been marginalized or have had to live out their love in secret, to have that love recognized by society. Until his death Father Pérotti was my secretary. He did not hide his homosexuality and was one of the founders of David and Jonathan, a Christian association for the recognition of homosexuality. I recently met the members of this group. I told them that I thought that the word "marriage" was too deeply embedded in the collective consciousness as meaning the union of a man and a woman to be rapidly assimilated for a union of people of the same sex. This could be unsettling and shocking for society. Why not use the word "alliance" which is just as beautiful but less marked by social usage?

The matter of the adoption of children is very complex and cannot be treated lightly. From among many points of view it seems to me that the most important is psychological reflection. We should listen to the psychologists and see if, in the long term, experience shows whether the fact of not having parents of differing sexes limits the child psychologically or socially. To me, this would be the most valid reason for forbidding homosexuals from bringing up children. We must learn whether being the child of same sex parents is some kind of handicap for the child – or too heavy a burden to bear. On the other hand, we know that having a heterosexual couple as parents is by no means a guarantee of happiness or stability for the child.

10. Should women be ordained priests?

Another contemporary social problem which comes up all the time and which is vital for the 21st century church is the role of women in Catholicism. As prefect of the Congregation for the Doctrine of the Faith, Cardinal Ratzinger slammed the door on all progress towards the ordination of women. Except for the matter of the ordination of married men, it is unlikely that Benedict XVI will do an about-turn on these questions. And this despite the fact that arriving at the highest office may change a man, liberating him and widening his vision.

I have never understood why John Paul II and Cardinal Ratzinger stated that the church would never ordain women. This affirmation implies that such a practice would be incompatible with the basis of the Christian faith. Yet those who have taken up this position, no matter how eminent the functions they hold, have never been able to put forward a single decisive theological argument that proves that the ordination of women would be contrary to the faith.

The main argument that is put forward is that Jesus chose no women among his apostles, although he had many women around him. I see this as a sociological and not as a theological argument. At the time, in Greek, Roman or Jewish society, it was the norm that women did not hold official positions. These customs, as we know, depended on a *macho* culture that was linked to the domination of the patriarchal system. Males were considered superior to women, more rational and alone capable of ruling or teaching.

In that context, it is difficult to see Jesus, no matter how free he was himself, going against a culture ingrained in all the peoples of the Mediterranean basin. This would have created incomprehension. But it is difficult today to see why the church should retain these prejudices since mentalities have greatly evolved on these matters.

Who could claim today that women are inferior to men or incapable of teaching or governing? In recent years there has been a real cultural revolution that has enabled numerous women to take up the highest responsibilities: we need only think of Indira Gandhi in India, Margaret Thatcher in Great Britain or Benazir Bhutto in Pakistan. As for theological education, for many years the Protestant faculties have shown us that they have excellent women theologians, both lay people and ordained.

In writing this I am not claiming that there are no ontological differences between men and women. I believe that women are often more compassionate, more intuitive, more sensitive and that men are more logical and good organizers. But these are not absolutes. There are many men who are intuitive and compassionate; there are very rational women who have remarkable administrative abilities. I cannot understand why such women who feel a vocation and who have the ability should be denied access to ordination.

There is one last argument used by the supporters of a male only priesthood – that Jesus was a man and that since the priest functions *in persona Christi* he must be of the same sex as the Christ. This argument is of the same level as the preceding one. The Christ as second person of the Trinity has no gender, either male or female. Jesus, as the incarnation of that divine person, could have only one sex. Taking into account, once again, the mentality of the time, it is difficult to see how a woman could have been taken seriously and secured the loyalty of a band of disciples, including women, who were filled with anti-feminist prejudice. It seems to me that the choice of gender for Jesus was one of convenience and not of theological necessity.

I believe that the question of the ordination of women is nothing more than a matter for the evolution of mentalities. It is probable that the church will evolve on this point in the coming years. I certainly hope so.

11. Mary Magdalene

When there is discussion about the role of women in the church, we automatically think about the special place that Mary Magdalene holds in the gospels.

Before I became a novice, when I was barely seventeen years old, I made a brief three-day retreat in a monastery near Grenoble. It was then that I found a short but very powerful passage in the gospels that has remained with me since. It is the meeting of Jesus and Mary Magdalene after the crucifixion.

In his gospel, John tells us that at dawn on the second day after the terrible sufferings of Jesus, Mary of Magdala went with some other women to embalm the body of Jesus. The stone was rolled aside, the tomb empty. For Mary it was appalling; who had taken away the body of her beloved? Not for one moment did she imagine the resurrection. In despair she looked everywhere for the corpse, to see and hold it for one last time. It was then that a man appeared in the garden who she could not see very well since she was preoccupied by the search for the body, and whom she took to be the gardener. Jesus, the risen Jesus, said to her: "Woman, why are you weeping? Who are you seeking?" Mary answered him: "If it is you who have removed him, tell me where you have left him so that I may go and take him."

Jesus then pronounced the simple word "Mary", and on hearing her name, Mary recognized him and her ears, her eyes and her heart were all opened to the mystery of the person of the resurrected Christ. She threw herself towards Jesus with a heartfelt cry: "Rabboni", a Hebrew word that might be translated as "beloved master". The closest disciples often called their master by a nickname which at the same time showed respect and deep affection. I remember that in India, the disciples of Gandhi called him "Gandhidji".

These two words that follow each other "Mary" and "Rabboni" profoundly moved me and continue to move me nearly eighty years later.

In these two words alone is contained the whole mystery of incarnation and redemption, the whole mystery of Christ. They show the passionate love of God for humankind. God calls each of us with great tenderness by our own name: "Mary". And human beings, when they recognize this passionate love of God, throw themselves towards God with equal fervour: "Rabboni".

I am deeply moved every time I read those two words. Deep inside myself I hear "Henri" (my baptismal name), and I feel the loving eyes of Jesus resting on me.

On the quays of the Seine in Paris there is shop called "Raboni" Each time I pass the big signs bearing its name, I cannot help trembling when I think about the word that Mary spoke. I intimately share the total joy of the person who finds his or her lover. It brings tears to my eyes and to my heart.

12. Did Jesus have a physical relationship with Mary of Magdala?

The global success of the novel *The Da Vinci Code* has made it fashionable to discuss the possibility of a marriage between Jesus and Mary Magdalene. From what I hear, this thesis has shocked many Christians and upset many more. I must admit that such a thesis, which it is legitimate to formulate but for which there is no evidence at all, does not in the least upset my faith. My faith is nourished through prayer and through the gospels and nothing leads me to believe that Jesus was married nor that he had a physical relationship with a woman.

Having said that, I can see no real theological argument that would prevent Jesus, the incarnate Word, from having a sexual experience. I am totally convinced that having taken upon himself full humanity he must have experienced sexual desire like everybody else. Did he want to satisfy this desire? If the answer is positive, then he must have lived through it in a shared relationship and Mary Magdalene seems to have been the woman closest to him with the exception of his mother. But it is also possible that he did not satisfy this desire, which would not have made him any less human.

In other words, I do not agree with those who say that Jesus could not have had sexual relationships because he was divine. But I also disagree with those who insist that because of his human nature he must have had sexual relations with a woman. It is clear to me that God incarnate could

know physical pleasure but also know desire without giving in to it. And in either case, nothing that
is essential to the Christian faith is changed.

13. Mary: mother of Jesus or idol?

What about the principal female character in the gospels, the mother of Jesus?

I am impressed by the recent accumulation of dogma concerning Mary, the mother of Jesus, and ask myself why this is so. The church is concerned certainly to respond to popular devotion and to underline the unique role of this woman. But that gives rise to two problems.

The first is that of dehumanization. Unlike her son who combined in himself human and divine nature, Mary possessed only human nature. She was a woman similar in being to all other women, though she had been chosen by God to carry the incarnate Word in her womb. This made her unique, but it would not distance her from us nor permit her to escape from the temptations and weaknesses of humanity. The doctrine of the Immaculate Conception, promulgated by the Catholic Church in 1845, stated that Mary carried no trace of original sin. In other words, she had a status unique among humans from the time of her conception. She was unlike other human beings – even the greatest saints – who all carry in their flesh the trace of original sin. I shall explain later why I am disinclined to believe easily in original sin. But even if original sin exists and is transmitted bodily from generation to generation since Adam and Eve, I do not see why Mary, who is wholly human, should have been privileged to avoid it nor in what way it would have been necessary for the realization of the mystery of incarnation. I see belief in the doctrine of the Immaculate Conception as distancing us from Mary.

Is it not the same for the doctrine of the Assumption of Mary, officially promulgated in 1950? According to this dogma, the body of Mary would not have known corruption but would have ascended to heaven, being transfigured in some way. Is this not another way of stripping Mary of her humanity by making her an incorruptible demi-god?

Let us guard ourselves against this rising danger of mariolatry. The first Christians struggled with all their force against paganism and idolatry to proclaim, like Jesus, that only God is to be worshipped. Adoration is only authentic and true if it leads to the infinite. To worship Mary or the saints is not worthy of a Christian.

I have a deep fondness for Mary the mother of Jesus. Every day I repeat the words of the *Magnificat*. I often include it in my prayers addressed to God. But I cannot accept the explicit worship of Mary, which for some people takes on more importance than worship of the Creator. That becomes idolatry. Should Mary take over the role of the goddesses of antiquity against whom early Christianity struggled so as to bring to the whole world the revelation of God, one and indivisible, and whom alone we may legitimately worship?

14. How can original sin be better defined in the light of science?

The idea of the Immaculate Conception leads us to one of the basic notions of Christian theology, that of original sin.

In our catechism lessons we were taught to read Genesis as a historical text: Adam and Eve were the first human beings and our ancestors. As a result of their sin, human nature has ever since been corrupted. All the vices and evils of humanity have their origin in this original sin.

Many theologians do not hesitate to quote a passage of St Augustine that is relevant to the misuse of a literal reading of Genesis. The text is in *De genesi ad litteram* and it says that it is a shameful and pernicious thing that a non-Christian should hear a Christian talking about holy scripture, describing idiocies in such a way that the unbeliever has trouble to keep from laughing. And when the non-Christian has heard such absurd things described in the Bible, why should he take seriously the texts concerning resurrection, hope of eternal life and the kingdom of heaven?

What St Augustine writes is even more important a thousand years later regarding the origin of man and the delicate subject of original sin.

Father Loewe, deeply committed to the evangelization of the working classes, wrote in his magazine *La mission ouvrière* that the first chapters of Genesis, which begin most catechisms, were a total disaster for children and parents. Who can be ignorant of the origins of mankind at the present time? It is in the programme of public elementary education. It is clear that in our time these texts from Genesis are to be seen as revealing the relationship of man to God, but not as a history book.

I was impressed to discover recently that Pope John Paul II had himself solemnly recognized the validity of the Darwinian theory of evolution. In a document that passes largely unnoticed, John Paul II adopted a very clear position when speaking to the Pontifical Academy of Science on 22 October, 1996. He began by noting that Pius XII, in an encyclical of 1950, already considered evolution as a serious hypothesis; he went on to say that today, fifty years later, new knowledge forces us to admit that evolution is more than a hypothesis. He noted that it is impressive that this theory has progressively imposed itself on the thinking of researchers after a whole series of discoveries made in different disciplines. The unprovoked and unsought convergence of results of independent scholarly investigations constitutes an important argument in favour of evolution.

John Paul II went on to say that the philosophical interpretation of these results could be very different. In a materialist perspective, it could be deduced that spirit could come out of living matter as an *epiphenomenon* of that matter. From a mystic standpoint one would insist on the "ontological leap" that constitutes the appearance of human consciousness and the capacity for symbolization that is unique to humankind (consciousness of mortality, art, and religion…)

The church accepts the fact that human beings appear at the end of a long physical and biological process following on from those of other living creatures. The only subject on which the church maintains a clear position is about the nature of human beings created in the image of God. Vatican II underlined that humanity "is the only creature on earth which God willed for itself", *Gaudium et Spes*, 24. Unlike all other living creatures, only the human is considered as an end in itself, a person, created, male and female, in God's image, through whose spirit they are able to experience the gift of self and to enter into communion with God. For the church it is thus all-important to maintain that if the human body has developed out of previously existing living matter, humanity's spiritual soul has been directly created by God. Therefore Christians insist on the ontological leap which is the appearance of humanity as a new being in the long evolutionary development with the characteristics of this new species, consciousness of self, reflection, moral conscience, freedom, ethical or religious experience, all qualities which are found only in humankind and which, according to the Christian faith, arise from the fact that humanity has a spiritual soul created by God.

The new *Catechism* of the Roman Catholic Church obviously deals with the question of original sin in different places. However, anyone who examines this problem will deeply regret that a more profound examination was not attempted in this catechism, which is being widely distributed.

Finally, how can I keep silent about the wish that I have had since my childhood – to substitute for the inadequate and unseemly words "original sin" the word "wound"? A wound that is not self-inflicted, but which preserves our innocence. Would it not be better to use the phrase "inherited wound"?

15. The genius of Teilhard de Chardin

In discussing the essential question of original sin and evolution, I should like to pay tribute to a man who was not only a scientist (a palaeontologist) but also religious (Jesuit) and who played a very important role in the twentieth century in reconciling the Christian vision with the scientific theory of evolution. His name was Pierre Teilhard de Chardin.

He was a close friend. I first heard of him at the age of fifteen when he came back from a long spell in China. Later, just after my escape to Algiers, a friend gave me a copy of the text of his book *Le Milieu divin*. His work has accompanied me ever since. I have just read his complete works and I am totally amazed by the mix of science, faith and mysticism.

I last met him shortly before his death. It was at St Germain-des-Prés, just after the war. I then lived in a ground floor flat between the two cafés *Les Deux Magots* and *Le Flore*. I held open house every Thursday evening. One evening I welcomed Teilhard with two other notable Christian philosophers, the Orthodox, Nicolas Berdiaev and the Catholic, Gabriel Marcel. The meeting was a total fiasco ! Teilhard died a few weeks later in New York on Easter Day, as he had wanted.

From his childhood, Teilhard de Chardin was fascinated by physical matter which, unlike many Christians, he did not see as the enemy of the spiritual. He became a famous scientist, specializing in fossils and in the history of the earth; at the same time he devoted his life to God. His audacious theses which try to reconcile evolutionary theory with Christian faith were badly received by the Catholic Church which accused him of pantheism. Yet he has always been defended by the greatest theologians like Father Henri de Lubac. For Teilhard, evolution has meaning and attains this in what he calls the "Omega" point, the Christ. His mystical vision is imbued with a poetic lyricism which irritates some people, but which I have always liked. I believe that ultimate truths can be expressed only as poetry.

16. Jesus, saviour of humanity

We must learn to consider the stories in Genesis as myths. The characteristic of myth is that it contains information that is not specifically in the narrative. There is meaning that is inherent. We must read the first chapters of Genesis in this ontological way. They tell us fundamental truths about mankind but have no value as history.

The central message contained in these stories is that all human beings, and not only our remote ancestors, tend to reject any dependence on divine authority. They want to be their own masters.

Through the medium of myth, the Bible reveals the profound truth that there have been continual ruptures between humankind and God. In wanting to be independent, human beings have moved away from the Father but have become a hostage to themselves. Human beings are no longer dependent on God but in the process become captive to themselves, prisoners of their egoism, instincts and passions. In wanting to be freed from being the servant of God, humanity has become enslaved.

By taking bodily form, Jesus offers the ransom which humankind must pay for freedom. Talking about himself, Jesus said that he did not come to be served but to serve "and to give his life as a ransom for many". The *many* represents the whole of humanity, not only one group or one people.

All through my life I have thought about this word "ransom". Who is paying the ransom? Who is demanding it?

There are two traditional theological explanations of this mysterious saying of Jesus, neither of which I find satisfactory.

It used to be said that sinful man was captive of the devil. Even in my childhood we used to be told that if you were very bad you would belong to the devil and end up in hell. But how can we imagine that Christ would give anything to the devil? That total goodness could pay anything to evil? This is nonsense.

Another theological tendency was to claim that the person paying the ransom was God. Offended by human sin, only an infinite offering could come up to the level of the sins committed so that only God could pay it by becoming incarnate. I find this explanation every bit as offensive as the first: it encourages suffering by emphasizing the expiatory sufferings of Christ. The more Jesus suffers, the more he pays for the offences of humanity and the more he contributes to humanity's ransom. It is frightful.

It was from passing a lot of time with drug addicts that a better explanation came to me. Addicts are their own torturers as well as being victims. They are both hostage and extortionist. Starting from this understanding I realized that it was the same for everyone. Being separated from our divine origin, we have become our own executioners. We are slaves to our passions and to our egocentricity.

In becoming human, Christ came to free us from ourselves. He offers us the possibility of reconnecting with the divine. He gives each of us the ransom with which we can free ourselves. To be Christian is to learn that Jesus has given us once again the possibility of loving in truth. And so we can dare to say the Lord's Prayer.

I shared my thoughts on ransom and original sin with Cardinal de Lubac shortly before his death. He strongly encouraged me to go on in this direction telling me that this method of explaining the word of Christ seemed to him to be correct and enlightening.

I do not pretend to be a great theologian but I hope that this meditation will make things clearer for people who believe and who ask questions about the mysterious words of Jesus and, on a wider level, about the mysteries of salvation.

17. Presence and absence of Jesus

I used to wonder why Jesus could not have stayed with us. Why couldn't he continue to perform miracles and to teach us? In the contemporary world with its powerful media, think what fantastic success he could have had! Far more than the most saintly and charismatic pope! Yet the danger of idolatry, already considerable with a pope like John Paul II, would have been too great. We would no longer be in intimate and interior communication with the Christ – we would be worshipping him as an idol exterior to ourselves. We would all want to see him, touch him and be healed by him, but without really hearing and thinking about what he has to say to us. On the other hand, he might be so impressive that he would terrify us. To enter into an intimate, interior and loving relationship with Jesus, and so through him with God, we must shut our eyes and listen with the heart.

This is certainly why the resurrected Christ did not linger on earth in an observable way. And this is why Jesus is not a shining and visible marvel two thousand years later. He is like the mist in the garden on Easter morning when he meets Mary Magdalene. He is as he was on the road to Emmaus. His closest friends and disciples did not recognize him because they were so absorbed in their own cares and sadness. Then, all of a sudden he pronounces a word – "Mary" – or performs an action, breaks the bread, and our eyes are able to see him.

He offers himself to us, but we can only meet him by listening in our hearts, through silent prayer. He continues to speak and act in every Christian who tries to follow in his steps.

Every time I meet a person who has been terribly hurt in this life, I hear Jesus call them by their name and I try to communicate through my voice, my look, my hands, what Jesus said with so much love: "Paul", "Jacqueline", "Francis", "Nathalie".

Christianity is the meeting of one person with another. It is the gospel which continues. Nothing else.

18. The eucharist, the heart of Christian communities

Jesus found a wonderful method of remaining with us discreetly, through the consecration of bread and wine that become for believers the presence of his body and blood.

Of all the sacraments, the eucharist is the most important. It is at the same time the testament of Jesus and the realization of his presence among us. It is the most important to me and that which touches me most deeply.

The eucharist is truly the sacrament of faith. Outside the Christian faith, it is only an insignificant piece of bread. With faith it is of supreme importance. There are various interpretations of the eucharist among Christians. For Catholics, it is the real and mysterious presence of Christ. In theological terms, according to St Thomas Aquinas, this is "transubstantiation". This is a rather barbaric word which means that the substance of the bread is transformed through the words of the priest into the substance of Jesus.

At the other extreme, most Protestants believe that the eucharist is a symbol, the consecrated bread is not the body of Christ, but the symbol of his presence among us.

Personally, like many Catholics and Protestants, I find myself in a median position. I am not concerned with "transubstantiation" but only with the PRESENCE. I believe, without knowing how, and without trying to find a rational explanation, that the Christ is mysteriously present in the consecrated host. No matter how.

Thus the eucharist sometimes brings a real presence of Jesus to believers. I have often sensed that great tenderness when praying for hours before the host displayed in a church. Many monks and nuns have a very deep experience of this tenderness. I remember having visited the shanty town of Tu Duc at Saigon in 1975. In the shacks lived families and a few nuns. While I was there the mother of a family asked one of the nuns, "Why are you always smiling when you have neither husband nor children?" and the nun answered spontaneously, "It is because I know that I am loved by him whom I love." This love, this tenderness of Jesus, is especially present for believers in the eucharist.

Perhaps the church has meaning only because it maintains the presence of the eucharist. It is its fundamental mission. Small, hidden and isolated Christian communities have been able to survive for centuries in certain countries of Asia thanks to the presence of the eucharist.

19. Returning to the Christianity of the early centuries

Throughout history, as a result of the confusion between spiritual and temporal power, the church has often revealed itself as quite odious. Popes became kings, sometimes more powerful than the monarchs of the major countries of Europe, and bishops became princes. This confusion comes from the fourth century under the rule of the Roman emperor Constantine. By making Christianity – hitherto persecuted – the official religion of the Roman Empire, he rendered a very bad service to the church.

Jesus insisted on the necessity of the separation of powers, "Give to Caesar what is Caesar's and to God that which is God's". He also refused to become the political leader whom his disciples expected. The early Christians remained faithful to this rule of separation of politics and religion that long afterwards would be called secular. Thus everything changed with Constantine and the church became a political power, wanting to rule society. This has been called Christendom.

Since the enlightenment and revolutions of the eighteenth and nineteenth centuries the church has lost its power and temporal influence. The Second Vatican Council (1962-5) not only noted this evolution but welcomed it as a way in which Catholics could re establish contact with evangelical values. I shall never forget the very true saying of Father Yves Congar when the Council opened, that "Vatican II will inaugurate the end of the Constantinian era".

This return to source is not yet achieved. The papacy is too powerful and still reflects the role of the pope/emperor. For instance, the pope is elected for life as were the emperors. The papacy should not be abolished, but it should become more modest.

The church must be liberated from the Roman predominance over all local churches and from its centralization of power and jurisdiction. This is one of the conditions necessary for making the church fully evangelical as well as for the reconciliation of all Christians in unity.

20. The gospels

It must be remembered that the gospels which describe the doings, the acts and the words of Jesus were not written by neutral observers. These are not journalistic reports but accounts written by believers who had lived, thought over and analysed these acts and words before putting them down in writing.

They are therefore the reflection of the faith of these first Christian communities and not always necessarily in accordance with historical fact. This explains, for instance, why certain accounts contradict others, like those of the meeting with and the calling of the first disciples. This should be a warning against taking these texts too literally.

I have a preference for John's gospel. Right from the start, "In the beginning was the Word", he leads the way in which my spiritual life has developed throughout three quarters of a century, the mystery of the incarnate Word. Redemption did not necessitate the suffering of Jesus, but the sole reality that the Word became incarnate. The scourging and the killing were not the will of God but the simple consequences of the divine decision of incarnation. The Word become flesh assumed the whole human condition.

21. The Holy Trinity

The mystery of the incarnate Word forms the heart of Christian revelation. It depends on another mystery, that of ONE God in three persons.

There is a constant thread to my spiritual life that has led me progressively to discover the mystery of ONE God in three persons. As a Franciscan novice, I found the Word of God who revealed himself to Moses through the burning bush, "You will say that I AM has sent you." After pantheistic ideas that resulted in the person of God disappearing, I had a real revelation in finding this saying: "I AM." I felt drawn to uniting with I AM.

Since then I have only been able to worship "O Thou who art, yes – be".

I at once associated I AM with love; I AM is loveable. The nature of love is to be generous of itself: by analogy it is the reason we call God "Father" as revealed to us by Jesus. God is father because God's being is love and love spreads spontaneously.

I am thus accustomed to living with the mystery of the Trinity: the Father giving of himself to the Word, which is to say the Word of the Eternal who proclaims "I am" and the Word giving himself to the Father. The Spirit comes from the love of the Father and the Word. Though it is incomprehensible to human intelligence, the mystery of One God and three persons does not shock me because

I can understand it in my heart. If God is Love, God can only be fruitful and this fruitfulness can be expressed only in the mystery of God's being.

22. Liberty and super-liberty

To my understanding, Christianity, following Judaism, is one of the religions that has most insisted on human freedom. This liberty is first seen in relationship with the Creator; people are always free to believe, or not to believe, to obey the commandments of God or to reject them. This freedom of conscience is fundamental. It is the essential condition of love. For if we are forced to love God, what value could that love have?

Yet there are two methods of forcing someone to love. One is a violent method, a sort of perverted affective manipulation which makes the other person totally dependent. This unfortunately often exists in human relationships, between parents and children or within couples. But there is another method which is more respectful of the other person: to reveal oneself as so good that they cannot help but love you. This is the reason why God created us while being hidden from us. We cannot see God. We can only know God indirectly. It is this essential obscurity which makes faith necessary. The whole greatness of humankind is to love God in faith, without touching, without seeing, without knowing God directly. Thus liberty is total.

This classical theological reflection on human freedom led me to consider the liberty of the divine persons when I was writing about the mystery of the Trinity. For instance, it is impossible that the Word should not be in agreement with the Father. The Word is necessarily free but is completely within the light of the Father. When I arrive in heaven, one of my first questions to God will be, "How is it that the three divine persons are never in disagreement?"

The mystery of the Trinity shows us therefore that there can be a form of liberty, which I shall call super-liberty, that is real yet renders us incapable of disagreeing and holding different opinions. I cannot restrain myself from asking why, if such a "super-liberty" exists within God, God has not given it to humanity, and why humanity has not been created with full awareness – which would have spared us our ancestral condition of futile suffering. Why do we only have a part of this awareness, this light?

23. Sin

A fundamental theological question, that of sin, must be reconsidered by the church. The existence of sin cannot be denied. It alienates human liberty and prevents humankind from being in touch with the deepest parts of their being, from true relationships with other people and with God. But we have insisted too much on sin being an act. We often hear "I have committed a sin" in confession, referring to a particular act. Yet it seems to me that what is much more important is not the act but the *habitus*, the repetition of the act.

The isolated act, a crime of passion, an adultery of a single night, is not the same as repeating an act which is harmful to oneself or to others. We have broken through a barrier and become accustomed to the situation. This is much worse and calls our freedom and our responsibility into question. The *habitus*, or repeated sin as it is called in theology, is much more serious than a single act.

It is important to remember this so as to remove guilt from people who transgress through anguish, an error of judgement or an uncontrollable urge but who afterwards exercise their liberty to make sure that they do not sin again. But it is also important to show those who get used to committing destructive acts that this is very serious and calls into question their moral responsibility.

We can then correctly use the term "vice". Just as virtue comes from the repetition of a good action – we are virtuous because we do good things – vice comes from the repetition of an evil action. Real sin that is vice is the installation of behaviour that is destructive of ourselves or others.

This does not mean that God cannot pardon the sinner, even the worst, since God alone can know our hearts and motivations and can know how far our liberty is altered or involved. Some people do not have sufficient will-power to be able to avoid committing evil that they would prefer to avoid. Others mechanically repeat an evil that they have suffered in their childhood. This is why Jesus told us, "Do not judge" long before Freud. But this is not a reason for not struggling with all our strength to avoid committing another act which we know will cut us off from what is noble and beautiful in us, which will cut us off from other people and, in the end, cut us off from Love.

24. Does hell exist?

Contrary to what many Christians think, no church council has ever said that hell exists. Christian preachers have often used the fear of hell to convert people, which seems to me to be a particularly bad method, but no evidence exists to show that it exists or, what comes to the same thing, that there is a single, damned soul within.

The more I think about the mystery of the God of Love, the more impossible I find it that any being, angel or human, who really knows the Deity, could freely reject God.

Theoretically, only a person who worships himself could reject the love of God, not needing anyone else. Hell could amount to that. Yet in practice I cannot imagine that a being in full possession of freedom of choice and with a clear vision of good and evil could choose evil. I think that only special circumstances, such as previous experience of evil, could explain the worst behaviour. But once such a link is broken, once conscience is cleared and liberty experienced, the attraction of goodness will be greater than all else. How could self-worship survive the fullness of God's light and love?

25. Historical revelation, invisible revelation

The slogan, "no salvation outside the church", which was much used in my childhood, always scandalized me. How could it be possible that a God of love would only reveal himself to the baptized, a tiny part of humanity, so that they should be the only ones to be saved? It is ridiculous!

So, for Christians, there must be two ways in which God is revealed. A visible explicit revelation, that of the Bible and of Jesus Christ. And another invisible and more mysterious revelation which has not been written down, which has no prophet, but which touches the hearts of all people to encourage them to do good to their neighbours, to choose good rather than evil, to serve others rather than themselves. This invisible revelation – that of the Holy Spirit? – inspires other religions as well as people without any religion. It is because of this revelation that all philosophies, religious or not, can proclaim: "You shall love" and place compassion as the greatest of virtues.

26. Religious fanaticism

When the last century came to an end, nobody could have feared or imagined what violence our world now suffers, violence that grows out of fundamentalist currents in each human religion. Every bomb that explodes, whatever its origin, but which proclaims "God wants it so" – all the blood spilt in the name of faith – scandalizes and horrifies us.

Terrorist actions shock us, but things can only get worse if we do not look seriously at the causes.

I have just reread an encyclopaedia on twenty centuries of Christianity, and I was struck by what the crusades really were. Using the pretext of liberating the holy places and permitting pilgrims to have access to them, a vast structure for domination was created that involved pillage and appalling massacres. The victims were not only the Arabs and Muslims but the Greek Orthodox with the terrible sack of Byzantium. Bitter memories of this period that lasted two centuries remain with the Muslims and also with Orthodox Christians.

The very idea of crusade, spilling blood to take over the places where Jesus lived, is simply repulsive. But to use this pretext for killing civilian populations with the clear aim of domination and accumulating wealth is even more so.

This is why I have serious doubts about the "crusade", the very word he used himself, which

George W. Bush is carrying out in the Middle East. There have been so many lies behind the fine words about the wish to bring freedom and democracy, so much blood of innocent civilians spilled, so many sordid economic and political calculations, that one cannot help thinking that history is, alas, repeating itself.

Should we have responded to the terrible provocation of Al Qaeda with a new crusade? Can we cure evil with evil? I fear that all this will propel the world into a new war between Christian and Muslim civilizations – which is, of course, what Bin Laden wants. Yet, with more wisdom and good sense, this conflict could well have been avoided.

Epilogue
Letter to God

Father,

I love you above all else.

Above all because you are he who can say I AM. And to have become aware of this when I was sixteen or seventeen years old means that, at ninety-three, I continue to live in this awareness.

I love you above all else.

Because:

- By sending Jesus, the Word, you show human beings who have always wanted to be sufficient unto themselves that they are insufficient.

- In a world that is focused on calculations and figures, in the eucharist you give us something stronger than doubt.

- In place of a suffocating atmosphere you send a breeze, the *spiritus* of the Holy Spirit who comes from the loving union of the Father and the Word together and in whom we live.

Yes, you are my love.

I have only been able to live this long because of my conviction that to die, whether one believes or not, is an encounter.

I love you above all else.

Yes, but… To be a credible believer, all those around me must know that I do not and will never accept the permanence of evil.

BEING, you are the master of the continuation or the ending of the existence of all that is.

Since you have the power to end all things, how may we comprehend that evil still exists? Does the prayer of Jesus not climax with the words "Deliver us from evil"?

Father, I thank you for helping me to refuse to "believe" as if I were indifferent to the perpetuation of evil in this world and in the next – that would be insincere.

Believing, loving, I can only be a believer "despite everything", that is to say, without understanding.

Too many people are ready to love you but are discouraged by this "despite everything". Have pity on them and have pity on the world.

Father, I have been waiting for so long to live completely in your PRESENCE which is, I have never doubted, "despite everything", LOVE.

October 4, 2005
Feast of St Francis of Assisi
Deo Gratias!

Abbé Pierre

Biographical note

Abbé Pierre, who was born in August 1912 and died at age 94 in January 2007, was one of the most widely recognized and popular spiritual leaders of France. A humble man committed to serving the poor, he received France's highest civilian honour. An objector to war and a proponent of peace, he participated in underground resistance to Nazi occupation. For six years following the war, this man of the church - at the encouragement of his archbishop - served as an elected member of the French parliament. The co-founder of the Emmaus movement providing community and housing for the homeless, Abbé Pierre was welcomed as a companion of popes, presidents, monarchs and such thinkers as Pierre Teilhard de Chardin, Albert Einstein, Camilo Torres and the Dalai Lama.

Originally named Henri Grouès, the future Abbé Pierre was born and raised in Lyon. In 1931 he joined the Capuchin monastic order under the name Brother Philippe, renouncing his inheritance and distributing his possessions to charity. The young monk's mentor was Father Henri de Lubac, a noted theologian and later a cardinal. In 1938, he was ordained to the priesthood and served his first charge in Grenoble until the outbreak of World War II.

In the initial years of the war, he became increasingly involved in aid to refugees and assistance to Jews and others in crossing French borders into neutral Switzerland and Spain. Working with the

French resistance from 1942, in 1944 he was arrested by German authorities but escaped and made his way to Algiers. At war's end, he was elected a deputy in the French parliament on a platform of aiding the destitute.

While working with refugees, Abbé Pierre had established a professional partnership with Mademoiselle Lucie Coutaz. In 1949, Abbé Pierre and Lucie Coutaz became co-founders of the Emmaus communities, calling upon youth to join in a struggle against extreme poverty. Beginning in France, the Emmaus movement and its mission of development and justice expanded across North Africa and the Middle East into countries throughout the world.

Wearing his customary cape and beret, Abbé Pierre became a striking and widely-recognized figure in France. He was the author and the subject of countless books and articles. His commentaries on faith and contemporary culture appealed to audiences due to their unexpected, inspiring and at times controversial content. In July 2004 he was awarded France's highest national recognition, the Grand'Croix de l'Ordre de la Légion d'Honneur. In bestowing the award, President Jacques Chirac described Abbé Pierre as "an extraordinary man, a figurehead who has devoted his life to the defence of the rights and dignity of the human individual."